Original title:
Life's Purpose: A Journey to the Unknown

Copyright © 2025 Creative Arts Management OÜ
All rights reserved.

Author: Isaac Ravenscroft
ISBN HARDBACK: 978-1-80566-292-1
ISBN PAPERBACK: 978-1-80566-587-8

Illuminating the Unknown

In the dark, a lightbulb flicks,
Chasing shadows, dodging tricks.
A map drawn with crayon and glee,
Turns out it leads to a giant bee!

With every twist, a giggle grows,
A penguin walking on his toes.
The path's a dance of silly plans,
Who knew adventure was made of pans?

The Heart's Unfinished Story

My heart writes tales on toilet rolls,
Of pizza parties and funky moles.
A chapter lost, an epic fail,
But laugh it off, that's the holy grail!

The ink may smudge when laughter's loud,
A trampoline in a sleepy crowd.
Each page a jump, a foolish quest,
In scribbled words, we find our rest.

Serpents of Doubt and Destiny

A serpent whispers in my ear,
"Try spaghetti!"—I quiver with fear.
Yet it slithers off with a cheeky grin,
While I chase my dreams, my head in a spin.

Doubt wears socks with sandals too,
A fashion choice I cannot construe.
But with a wiggle, a jolly spin,
I'm off to chase the zany win!

Tides of Uncertainty

Waves of doubt crash on the shore,
When should I leave? Or stay for more?
A surfboard made of hopes and dreams,
Rides through oceans of giggles and screams.

The tide rolls in, and then it's out,
What should I do? I scream and shout.
But with each splash, a dance I see,
Uncertainty's just fun in disguise, whee!

Flickers of the Eternal Quest

In search of a goal with a map of spaghetti,
Fumbling through options, it all feels confetti.
Chasing cloud dreams, like chasing a cat,
Every turn takes me to the land of the brat.

With each step forward, a slip on a shoe,
I wonder if life's just a game of peekaboo.
The snails pass me by, they're leading the race,
I'm over here tripping on my own shoelace.

Trails through the Heart's Wilderness

In dense woods of wonder, I wander around,
Looking for wisdom but lost and spellbound.
Trees whisper secrets, but I can't quite hear,
Is that a wise owl, or just my dinner near?

I brought a compass, it spins like a top,
And here's my fine map, which leads me to shop.
Following paths under very strange lights,
I find all the answers, but none fit just right.

Amongst the Stars of What Lies Ahead

I stargaze for answers, but see only dots,
They giggle and dance, distracting my thoughts.
I ponder the cosmos, is it all just a game?
Or a cosmic joke, where we're all just the same?

A comet zips by, with a trail made of glee,
I wave at a nebula, it waves back at me.
Galaxies swirl with the greatest of ease,
While I trip on my dreams and lose track of the bees.

The Secrets the Wind Whispers

The wind carries laughter, or maybe a joke,
Blows past me briskly, like a dog with a cloak.
It whispers of mysteries, both silly and grand,
While I chase down the tales, tripping in the sand.

A gust pulls my hat to a place far away,
Where laughter is currency, and silliness stays.
With every soft breeze that tickles my ear,
I ponder if purpose is sipping a beer.

Forging Through the Fog

With my compass spinning round,
I tripped over a sleeping hound.
Lost my map, but hey, that's fine,
I'll just follow this great wine.

Clouds above look like a mess,
My directions? A big guess.
But hey, let's dance through this haze,
Who needs clarity, anyway?

The Dance of Uncertainties

I've got two left feet in a jig,
With each step I feel like a pig.
Twirl around, avoid that wall,
Oops! I think I just hit Paul.

The rhythm's a tricky friend,
Waltzing close to the world's end.
But laughing loud takes the lead,
Ballet shoes? I'll take a bead.

Serendipity on the Edge of Fear

Peered over the edge of my couch,
Found a snack, and a new pouch.
With pizza slices in my grasp,
I face the unknown with a gasp.

What lies beyond this comfy seat?
Maybe socks that don't match my feet.
But the thrill is a kick in the rear,
Bring on the popcorn, bring on the cheer!

The Road Less Roamed

I took a map, folded it wrong,
Ended up at a karaoke song.
They call it 'the road less roamed',
I think it's where my confidence's homed.

With a mic in hand, I croon and sway,
A few cringe, but it's okay.
For lost in the laughter and song,
I've found where I truly belong.

Steps into the Unfamiliar

With every step, I trip and fall,
Yet laughter echoes through it all.
I dance with socks that do not match,
In this odd game, I make a catch.

Each corner turned, a new surprise,
A duck with shades, oh how it flies!
The world is weird, and I'm its fan,
Who knew that fun was the whole plan?

I juggle dreams like fruits on strings,
Sometimes they crash; what joy it brings!
An alien once asked for a ride,
I laughed so hard, I barely cried.

So here's to paths we've yet to tread,
With wobbly legs and thoughts in our head.
The map is blank, but I won't fret,
For chaos is where we laugh, I bet!

The Compass of Desire

My compass spins, oh what a sight,
It points to pizza, late at night.
A slice in hand, I steer the course,
Through starry skies, I feel the force.

I crave adventures, wild and bold,
Yet find old socks and tales retold.
With ice cream dreams, I chase the dusk,
Pursuing wishes, oh so brusque.

The needle spins, it makes no sense,
Is this the way or just immense?
But with a grin, I take the leap,
For mischief's whispers, they don't sleep.

With every turn, I learn to sway,
My heart's desire guides the play.
So here we go, with zest and cheer,
In the night's quilt, I hold it dear!

Unwritten Maps of the Heart

In jest I scribble on my chest,
A roadmap made of doodles, blessed.
With arrows pointing everywhere,
And coffee spills, a hopeful flair.

A treasure hunt for socks mislaid,
Each step is fun; anxiety delayed.
The heart's a joker, plays its part,
With every giggle, it beats smart.

Imagine routes of ice cream trails,
With marshmallow clouds and chocolate gales.
For every wrong turn, a laugh we find,
Maps of joy, they're intertwined.

So I'll explore this canvas wide,
Painting dreams where wonders hide.
With silly steps and hearts so free,
We'll navigate this mystery!

Chasing the Mirage of Tomorrow

I chase a shadow down the street,
It giggles, runs; what a fun feat!
Morning coffee spills on my shoe,
I laugh, I dance, that's what I do.

The future shimmers, a mirage bright,
Like jellybeans in the morning light.
I skip and hop, it's never clear,
But with each tumble, I shed a tear.

Tomorrow's whispers call my name,
Yet all I find is sticky fame.
With marshmallow clouds, I float and glide,
In the circus of dreams, I take pride.

So here I am, a silly blob,
Transforming life with each small job.
Embracing chaos, the joy I borrow,
In this hilarious chase for tomorrow!

Beneath the Starlit Path

Underneath the twinkling night,
I lost my shoe, what a sight!
Stars are laughing, what a mess,
Maybe life's a game of chess.

Wandering what's beyond the hill,
My socks are damp, another thrill!
Picking daisies for my snack,
Oops, I tripped, and here's a crack!

The moon is winking, drawing near,
I hope it hides my silly fear.
Adventure calls with giggles sweet,
Even if I miss my feet!

Chasing shadows, off I go,
Where to next? I do not know!
Just following this pesky breeze,
And hoping I don't trip on leaves!

The Silent Call of Adventure

A squirrel talks, or so I think,
With all its nuts, it's hard to blink.
Shall I follow, chase it down?
Hey, look, it's wearing a crown!

The path ahead is full of turns,
A Google map? Nah, who returns?
With breadcrumbs tossed to mark my way,
Oh wait, a bird just ate my pay!

With every footstep, laughter flows,
"Where we're going?" nobody knows.
Mushrooms sprout, all shapes and sizes,
Could they be hiding some surprises?

Let's dance with raindrops, twirl around,
The moonlight's got me feeling crowned.
So if you see me slip and fall,
Just laugh and join me, that's the call!

Unfolding the Tapestry of Existence

Life's a quilt of patchy themes,
I thought I'd catch it in my dreams.
But fabric's tangled, colors clash,
I quilted over my favorite stash!

Twirling yarns with thoughts that twist,
"Is this a scarf or a cat?" I insist.
Frog jumped in, it made a splash,
Now this tapestry is quite brash!

Knitting needles flying far,
Who knew my muse was a shooting star?
Unraveled thoughts, like threads that stray,
With every tug, they run away!

So gather 'round for stories told,
Of tangled paths and dreams of gold.
The mess I've made, a lovely trace,
A journey every time, just a different face!

Finding Light in the Dark

In shadows deep where feelings creep,
I fumbled round, not one to keep.
My flashlight died, the ghost did laugh,
"Let's play hide and seek, you daft!"

There's something lurking, I can feel,
A sneaky cat looks too surreal.
With whiskers twitching, up it pranced,
In the dark, I swear it danced!

When clouds roll in and dreariness clings,
I just pretend to have wings.
If I'm a bird, I'll soar so high,
But I'll likely trip on my own tie!

So when it's dark and all seems lost,
Look for a laugh, it's worth the cost.
For in the twilight's silly dark,
Laughter glows, like a little spark!

In Search of Forgotten Dreams

I set out to find my lost sock,
In a land where mismatched shoes talk.
The map showed an X on a pile of fluff,
Where dreams hide, all blurry and tough.

I met a bird with an attitude flair,
Who chirped, 'Dream big, but do beware!'
It laughed at my goals like they were a joke,
Then flew off to dance with a big, furry bloke.

I chased after hopes through alleys of doubt,
Kicking around all the what-ifs about.
Found a treasure chest filled with my fears,
Got a gold medal for my wasted years!

At last, I tripped on a forgotten shoe,
Winked at my dreams, and said, 'Who are you?'
Together we laughed as we tripped down the lane,
In search of laughter, that glorious gain.

Threads of the Unknown

In a world spun from odd bits of thread,
I crafted a scarf for the things that I dread.
Each knot tied with worry, each fringe full of fright,
Fashionable fears, all wrapped up tight.

As I wandered through meadows of denim and lace,
A squirrel in a hat said, 'You're losing your pace!'
I asked him for wisdom, he gave me a nut,
"Sometimes you must dance, even when in a rut."

The fabric of life is a tapestry grand,
With stitches of laughter and a loom that won't stand.
I tripped on an ember, wore it like a crown,
Floated through worries that tried to bring me down.

So I'll weave all my dreams with humor and cheer,
Threading the unknown without any fear.
With each silly yarn, I'll create my own path,
Sprinkling joy like a fabric of laughs!

Echoes of a Wandering Soul

Through valleys of giggles and mountains of fun,
I roam with my thoughts, just me and my pun.
Each echo that bounces, a joke in the air,
A reminder that wandering requires some flair.

I met a lost echo who couldn't find home,
Claiming it traveled and never would roam.
I offered it popcorn and a seat by my side,
Together we laughed at the twists of the tide.

The world was a dance floor, with rhythms so bright,
Laughter my compass, my soul's guiding light.
Each step that I took led to a chuckle or two,
Entwined with the echoes, old friends where they flew.

So here's to the wandering, the giggles we share,
The whispers of silliness hang in the air.
Each echo a story, a journey defined,
In the hilarity of being, true freedom we find.

The Horizon Beckons

The horizon glimmers, it winks and it wobbles,
Calling me over with promises and gobbles.
I packed my suitcase with hope and some snacks,
Wrote a note for the socks hiding in the cracks.

As I marched toward tomorrow, the sun in my face,
A chicken with manners joined me in this race.
It clucked out a rhythm, a beat oh so grand,
To which I just danced, my destiny planned.

The winds were quite cheeky and played with my hair,
As I leaped toward horizons, not a worry nor care.
Sometimes I tripped on the path that I chose,
But laughed as I landed, my socks mismatched prose.

Every corner I turned seemed to giggle and grin,
Adventures awaited, let the fun times begin!
So here's to the horizon, the unknown so sweet,
With laughter as my guide, I'll dance on my feet!

Rivers of Possibility

In a boat made of dreams, we float,
With paddles of laughter, we gloat.
Sailing past shores of doubt—huzzah!
Oh, look! A fish wearing a straw hat, ha!

We dip our toes in waters so wide,
Splashing the doubts that try to hide.
The current pulls us, but what the heck,
We'll just float on this wild, silly trek!

A compass? Nah, that's just for maps,
We follow the giggles, not the traps.
Each wave that rolls has a joke to tell,
Especially that wave who tripped and fell!

So here we go, with buoyant zest,
Through rivers where laughter is truly blessed.
We'll laugh till we drop, come join the spree,
In this boat of wonder, so wild and free!

The Odyssey Never Ended

Packing snacks for a trip unknown,
My sock puppet's now my travel throne.
Wanderlust whispers, 'Just take a snack!'
At least I won't be hungry on this track!

With sandals on my feet that squeak and squeal,
I trip on purpose; that's part of the deal.
The map? Oh please, it's overrated,
I'd rather be lost, than feel related!

I call the wind my quirky guide,
It tickles my hair; oh, how it pried!
Every twist and turn is a chance to dance,
With a cabana of cactus—life's little romance!

So onward I march, with a silly grin,
Collecting odd trinkets and stories to spin.
An odyssey? Sure, but make it a game,
For each step I take is never the same!

Reflections on a Starlit Sea

Under the stars, we dare to dream,
Surfing on giggles and whipped cream.
The moon grins down; it's a silly sight,
As dolphins dance, wearing shoes that are tight!

The waves whisper secrets, splash and laugh,
Telling tall tales of a surfboard giraffe.
We sail with the jellybeans, swaying so free,
While octopuses juggle, oh, what a spree!

But wait! I think I've lost my phone,
It fell to the depths; it's a silly loan.
The seals roll their eyes, and what do they see?
A fish taking selfies, oh dear, oh me!

A voyage at sea that bends with delight,
Where every horizon is just out of sight.
In starlit waters, we twirl and we dart,
Painting our journeys on the canvas of art!

Notes from the Edge of Perception

At the edge of my mind, a parade unfolds,
With thoughts like popcorn, all glistening gold.
A chicken in a tux walks right by,
Saying, 'Why did I cross? Just to try!'

My pen writes notes, but they giggle and squirm,
Each word a twinkle, a jump, a worm.
I scribble a doodle of upside-down glee,
And my cat slaps the paper—oh, clever she!

Elusive ideas that slip through my grasp,
Like balloons in a storm, oh, how they clasp.
They swirl in the air, twist and then shout,
'Chase us! We're free! Come figure us out!'

So here I sit at the quirky fringe,
With nonsense and whimsy I gladly cringe.
On the edge of it all, I find my delight,
As the notes from my mind take off into flight!

Fragments of the Unwritten

I set out with snacks and a grin,
A map of spaghetti, where to begin?
With each twist and turn, I misplace my keys,
Lost in a world full of puddles and bees.

My compass points north, but I wander south,
Chasing my dreams with a cookie in mouth.
Each step that I take leads me further away,
To places where socks dance and marbles just play.

I meet a wise turtle who's stuck in a race,
He tells me, 'Slow down, it's not a fast chase.'
We laugh at the stars, they're so far and bright,
Even they probably get lost at night.

So off I continue, with chocolate and cheer,
To find what I seek, or at least grab a beer.
With friends by my side, I can gallivant,
In this grand adventure, there's no need to chant.

The Unknown Beckons

I woke up one day with a map made of toast,
It leads to a land where confusion's the host.
I pack up my socks, oh, which pair to choose?
The polka dots wink, while the stripes just snooze.

I trip over thoughts that have ten feet of hair,
They giggle and tug, oh, they want me to share.
With sandwiches falling from clouds up above,
I dance with the pickles, they're all kind of tough.

An owl in a bowtie offers me fries,
But no one knows how they made it to the skies.
I ask him for wisdom, he just hoots and spins,
Then flies off with a burger, oh where do I begin?

But onward I trot, with ketchup for luck,
Embracing the nonsense, as I'm quite the duck.
In this world of the strange, I find a bright hue,
With laughter and friendship, I'll always break through.

Along the Edge of Existence

At the edge of a cliff, I find my old shoe,
A relic of adventures that I never knew.
With a tutu of clouds, I twirl with delight,
Gazing at penguins who frolic in flight.

I check my reflection in puddles of cream,
There's a fish in a top hat, or so it would seem.
He winks and he whispers, 'Don't take life too keen,
Jump in with a splash; be goofy and green.'

A seagull named Larry steals fries from my hand,
He tells me a tale of a faraway land.
He claims that it's sunny where all the pigs dance,
But by now, I think I'll just give it a chance.

So I stagger and laugh, while tripping on glee,
With a hat made of jelly, I shout out my plea.
Let's ride on this wave, let's flip and just sway,
The edge looks much better when you're silly all day.

Mapping Dreams in the Dark

In the dark of the night, with a spoon for a guide,
I map out my dreams where the silly things hide.
With jellybean stars lighting paths in my head,
I'll untangle the noodles from my dreams in bed.

I stumble on shadows that wear silly hats,
They giggle and whisper like cheeky old cats.
Balloons made of wishes float high out of reach,
But who needs a plan? Just enjoy the peach.

A raccoon with glasses reads books upside down,
He claims he's a scholar, the king of the town.
He offers me nutmeg and says, "Take a hike,"
While juggling acorns, he laughs like a tyke.

So I scribble my thoughts with a crayon of joy,
Creating a map that each beast can enjoy.
In this world of the strange, what could go awry?
With laughter and dreaming, we'll always fly high.

Colors of the Great Unknown

In a world of vibrant hues,
I wear mismatched socks today.
With every step my color cues,
Guide me in a funny way.

Pinks and greens collide with glee,
Like clowns at a job interview.
Dancing through the mystery,
Twirling in a paint rendezvous.

A canvas stretched on wobbly frames,
Each splash is one grand joke.
I'm painting over all my aims,
With laughter's brushstroke poke.

Oh, the colors I can find,
In places no one dares to roam.
I chuckle as I lose my mind,
In this wild and chaotic dome.

The Compass of the Heart

My heart's a compass, true and bold,
With directions quite confused.
It points to candy shops of gold,
And gigs where I get bruised.

North is where the laughter leads,
But East has tasty pizza pies.
The South is sown with goofy seeds,
While West, well—that's just fries!

I follow instincts, pull the dial,
Where whimsy takes the wheel.
Each errant step sparks a smile,
As new adventures reel.

So here I dance, with map askew,
In this circus of the heart.
With every detour, something new,
A sweet and silly art.

Echoes of Tomorrow's Promises

Tomorrow's echoes softly sing,
Of cupcakes and roller coasters.
They whisper dreams of random things,
Like singing with flaming roasters.

Promises float on jellyfish wings,
In oceans of unexpected fun.
Like wearing socks while on swings,
Or running from a sneaky bun.

I'll chase those echoes without fear,
On wobbly stilts, I'll prance and play.
A jiggle here and giggle there,
While scouting treasures on display.

So let them call me what they will,
A jester with a future bright.
I'll echo back my joyous thrill,
And dance with every bit of light.

Shifting Sands of Purpose

In desert dunes where laughter rolls,
The grains of time shift left and right.
I build my castles with my goals,
But watch them tumble in the night.

Purpose runs from clumsy feet,
A mirage of ice cream treats.
As I chase it down the street,
I discover surprises sweet.

With each grain tossed, a giggle stirs,
Like camels who wear polka dots.
With shifting sands and silly blurs,
I laugh at all the tangled knots.

So I embrace the swirls of fate,
With every tumble, twist, and bend.
This journey's filled with laughs, innate,
A sandcastle dream without an end.

Whispers of the Uncharted

In the woods where squirrels conspire,
Lost maps lead us in circles dire.
We dance with shadows, skip on stones,
Chasing laughter, ignoring groans.

A cat with glasses reads a book,
Telling tales with a funny hook.
The wind sings tunes of distant lands,
While we make castles out of sands.

Elves sell cupcakes, trolls sell pies,
Both insist the secret lies,
In buttercream and icing swirls,
Mixed with giggles, pearls, and twirls.

So here we wander, quirks in tow,
With mismatched socks and faces aglow.
Through unknown paths we'll roam and play,
Laughing all troubles away, hooray!

Paths Beyond the Horizon

We stepped outside, what a surprise,
The sun had hatched its morning fries.
The flowers giggle, the birds take pause,
As we pause to ponder our own flaws.

A cow on roller skates zooms by,
We stop to wave, oh my, oh my!
With every turn, strange sights we see,
It's not just you and not just me.

The road is bumpy, full of traps,
Perhaps it's all a game of laps.
A sign that reads "Beware the ducks!"
We chuckle and dodge, full of plucks.

Through fields of giggles, we will race,
Chasing smiles in this funny place.
With every twist, a lesson waits,
And laughter now, it dominates!

Embracing the Unseen

Invisible things have the most flair,
Like socks that vanish, why do they care?
We embrace the weird, the wacky too,
With secret handshakes and a random stew.

A gnome offers wisdom, but it's just a prank,
Life's like a treasure chest, in fish tanks.
We frolic in mismatched shoes,
Under the moon, sharing our blues.

We climb high trees, mind the bees,
Making wishes with a silly breeze.
Every search leads us on a chase,
For fortune hides in the funny place.

So we leap into days yet unmade,
Armed with bubblegum and silly jade.
With each step, we'll depend on cheer,
For strange adventures bring us near.

The Quest for Meaning

Once upon a time, a knight so bold,
Questioned a muffin, and the tales it told.
With a sword made of frosting, and armor thin,
He sought the meaning, but lost his kin.

The dragon turned out to be just a cat,
Who offered him tea, and a comfy mat.
Together they laughed at the quest so grand,
While jellybeans rained, all across the land.

A wizard tripped over his floppy hat,
Cursing the day he learned to chat.
He claimed to know the answer true,
But slipped on his wand, falling askew.

In this journey where we frolic and flop,
The search for wisdom, we never stop.
For amidst the giggles and silly schemes,
Laughter grows, and fills our dreams!

Echoes in the Abyss

In the deep where secrets sway,
I tripped over a dolphin's play.
It squeaked and laughed, what a sight!
I asked, 'Is this how you take flight?'

With each turn, more giggles rise,
A cactus wearing tiny ties.
He winked at me, and I just grinned,
'You're sharper dressed than I've ever sinned!'

A fish on a skateboard zooms past,
'Catch me if you can!' he said, fast.
I slipped, I fell, what a fake
While he laughed—a silly mistake!

Yet in the swirl of giggly cheer,
I found my thoughts both bright and clear.
Sometimes it's absurd, and that's just fine,
In this kooky ride, I'll sip my wine.

Shadows of the Unfathomed

In the dark, a shadow danced,
Wore a top hat, and I was pranced.
'Care to join my waltz, dear friend?'
Said he with a grin that would not end.

Around we twirled through cosmic dust,
With rubber chickens, oh, what a bust!
We giggled at the stars that sneezed,
Each twinkle now a shimmering tease.

And then a chair, misplaced in space,
Sat upon by a croissant's grace.
'Pastry wars?' I chuckled and said,
'This galaxy's baked, let's feast instead!'

From shadows sprung laughter, both loud and bright,
As we danced away the shadowed night.
In every corner, a delight to find,
And blissfully lost, the best of kind!

Navigating the Infinite

On a boat made of cookies, I set sail,
The ocean giggling, a talking snail.
He said, 'Hold tight, or you might slide,
These waves are crunchy—let's take a ride!'

Navigating maps of jellybeans,
We dodged marshmallow pirates—sweet fiends!
'At the next skittle island,' he pointed with glee,
'We'll trade for a treasure—come sail with me!'

Through chocolate rivers, we bravely strode,
A caper-filled journey, adventures bestowed!
With laughter a-plenty, and splashes of jam,
I lost track of time, like a clueless yap.

We landed on shores made of meringue,
With cupcakes cheering, they began to sang.
In the embrace of sugary zest,
I found sweetness where I'd sought the best!

Beyond the Veil of Certainty

Behind the curtain of what we know,
A jester popped out, stole the show.
'Why so serious?' he quipped with ease,
'Let's juggle our doubts like squirrels in trees!'

Through veils of questions, we pranced and leapt,
With answers that peeked but rarely crept.
'Is it a mystery, or just a joke?'
I sighed, feeling light, like a freshly broke.

Past the what-ifs, we cascaded bright,
With rubber chickens appearing in flight.
'Lessons are fun if you let them be,
Like riding a rollercoaster, you'll just see!'

So here's to laughter, and silliness too,
In the unknown, where we forge something new.
With each chuckle, I found a way,
Beyond the veil, let's dance and play!

The Dance with Destiny

In shoes too big, we trip and sway,
Destiny giggles, come what may.
With every misstep, we find our groove,
Silly twirls that make us move.

A partner's laugh, a wink in the air,
As we fumble through, we hardly care.
Spinning in circles, we laugh and fall,
Oh, what a dance! We've all got a call.

Around the floor, we spin and glide,
With ice cream cones stuffed deep inside.
The music's loud, our hearts are light,
We'll dance 'til dawn, it feels so right!

With each quick step, there's room to play,
Socks on the floor, we slide away.
Embracing quirks, it's all a game,
Here's to our dance, and to mischief's claim!

A Symphony of Uncertainty

In a band with pots and pans galore,
We play a tune, then drop to the floor.
Each note's a quirk, a twist in the tale,
  We laugh so hard, we start to wail.

A trumpet blast, what's that, you say?
  It's just the cat— she's gone astray!
Tunes may be off, but spirits are high,
We'll serenade bats and the nearby pie!

Chorus of hoots, and squeaks that blend,
A symphony where the fun won't end.
With every wrong key, we find our cheer,
Sing it out loud, let the world draw near.

In our odd orchestra, we're all a part,
Each wobble makes a quirky start.
Life's offbeat rhythm keeps us on track,
Who needs a score? We'll never look back!

Whispers of the Untraveled Path

Down the lane where wild things play,
Whispers tell tales, come what may.
With a map all wrinkled and covered in grease,
We're off on a quest, searching for peace.

Through the brambles, we laugh and shout,
What's this— a sign? Or just a route?
A squirrel darts past, steals my snack,
An unplanned adventure, there's no turning back!

With every step, our doubts do fade,
Maybe we're lost, but hey! We parlay.
Through thorns and meadows, we stumble and skip,
Each stumble's a story; it's part of the trip.

By the river, the sky starts to glow,
We toast our mishaps, what do we know?
No right or wrong in this joyous maze,
Each twist and turn earns our bright praise!

Echoes in the Abyss

Diving deep where shadows play,
Echoes call, 'Come on, let's stay!'
With giggles and gurgles, we splash around,
Making waves where wonders abound.

Bubbles rise like dreams on high,
We'll chase the depths and giggle, oh my!
In the darkness, our laughter rings,
Who knew the abyss could bring such bling?

With jellies and fishes, we wade through glee,
Discovering treasures, just you and me.
No direction needed, just follow the sound,
In the abyss, where fun knows no bound!

So here's to the depths and the silly in town,
Echoes of giggles as we swirl around.
Adventure awaits in the wild unknown,
In every splash, we've truly grown!

Seeds of a Daring Journey

In the garden of dreams, I plant my fears,
Watered with laughter, not heavy tears.
The weeds say 'stop!' but I dance in delight,
With sunflowers winking at every night.

I pack my bags with jellybeans bright,
Map drawn in crayon under moonlight.
Each step I take in mismatched shoes,
Chasing rainbows, oh, what do I lose?

The path is a riddle, a puzzle to tease,
With squirrels as guides, if I only please.
They chatter in codes, I nod with a grin,
They might just show me where stories begin.

Oh, seeds of adventure, how wild you grow,
In the dance of the breeze, I twirl to and fro.
With giggles as fuel, I'm ready to roam,
Who knows what strange wonders will feel like home?

Wings of the Unexplored

I found a pair of wings, bright pink and blue,
With glittery sparkles, they shimmer anew.
I strapped them on tight, feeling quite bold,
And off I took to the skies, unconsoled.

A bird with no chart, I zigzagged about,
Through clouds made of candy, oh, what a rout!
I met a wise owl who said with a smirk,
"Direction is nonsense, just let yourself lurk!"

Through valleys of giggles and mountains of jest,
I fluttered past llamas who put me to test.
They played hopscotch with wisdom, oh what a sight,
With each silly jump, they brightened my flight.

So here I now soar, with a heart full of glee,
Chasing the quirks of what's yet to be.
With wings made for laughter, I'll never be bound,
In the air of the unknown, my joy shall be found.

Riddles in the Mist

There's a fog in my brain, a maze of delight,
Where riddles are tricky, all painted in white.
"Why did the chicken?" I ponder with glee,
"Perhaps it was searching for something like me!"

A shadowy figure offers me tea,
With answers in riddles as cryptic as me.
The more that I sip, the deeper I dive,
In this whimsical world, I feel so alive!

With foghorns of laughter ringing out clear,
I dance with the echoes, and erase all my fear.
Each twist of the mist brings a giggle or two,
It's puzzles and laughter; what else could I do?

Riddles are treasures, all wrapped up and snug,
Each one a tickle, a soft little hug.
So let's wander together, through shadows and light,
Where laughter's the answer, and joy takes flight.

The Fringe of Awareness

On the edge of the world, I peek and I play,
With a hat full of questions, I'm ready for sway.
Confetti of thoughts swirls bright in the air,
As I step on the fringe, without any care.

What if I'm wrong? What if I'm right?
A jester in shadows, I dance out of sight.
The universe chuckles, it teases my mind,
As it stretches and giggles, so joyfully blind.

With socks that don't match and shoes made for fun,
I sprint through the twilight, I bounce like the sun.
Each thought a balloon, drifting high above,
Fueling my voyage with laughter and love.

So here's to the fringe, let's take it today,
With a wink and a grin, we'll wander and sway.
In the glow of the zany, we'll frolic and roam,
For in this wild journey, we've already found home.

Flickering Lanterns in the Dark

In the night, we see them glow,
Flickering brightly, just to show.
Follow the light, but don't lose your shoe,
Who knew adventure could be so askew?

Beneath the stars where the wild things play,
Chatter and laughter lead the way.
Lost my map, but that's okay,
We'll find our path, come what may!

A journey we seek, with snacks in hand,
Finding weird creatures in this strange land.
With whispers of mischief, we'll make our stand,
Out here, we're a quirky band!

So grab your lantern, let's not delay,
Into the unknown, we laugh and sway.
What's waiting ahead, no one can say,
But we'll find joy, come what may!

Rising Tide of the Unknown

With waves of whimsy, we take the plunge,
Noses in the air, oh, the fun won't lunge!
Surfing on chaos, we're never on edge,
Though the depths below might be a bit dredged!

Floats of confusion bob all around,
We paddle and splash, with laughter profound.
What lies beneath? We've yet to be found,
Oh dear, is that a crab? With a frown?

Currents are tricky, but hey, we don't mind,
We'll ride the tide of the silly and blind.
On this kooky venture, together we're twined,
Exploring the strange, our fears left behind!

So we raise our hands, as the tide cranks it up,
With giggles and splashes, we fill every cup.
Unknowns await, but here we'll erupt,
In the rising tide, we dance and sup!

Emersion into the Mystery

The morning sun eats up the dew,
With coffee in hand, we're feeling brand new.
Off to explore, oh where shall we go?
Into the unknown, just follow the flow!

A squirrel in a hat greets us with cheer,
"Come, take a gander! The adventure is near!"
With snacks in our pack and no need for fear,
We forge on ahead, our mission is clear.

Past bushes and trees, with a skip and a hop,
We've lost all our worries; they've gone to the shop!
With shadows of laughter, we'll never stop,
Down paths where the kooky gnomes swap and bop!

So here's to the quest, with giggles galore,
To embrace every mystery, and come back for more!
Each twist and each turn, we dance, we explore,
In the world of wonder, who could ask for more?

Horizons of Untold Stories

In the distance, horizons peek out,
Stories await, with a dash of doubt.
With a luggage of giggles, we set out to roam,
To find tales hidden far from our home.

Wandering past gardens, where frogs sing to trees,
Collecting all wonders, along with the bees.
Each nook brings a chuckle, like whispers of keys,
Unlocking the fun, with the greatest of ease.

We've tripped over dreams, tasted goofy treats,
Met neighbors who speak in far-out tweets.
With every strange corner, adventure repeats,
Creating a symphony of life's wild beats!

So let's raise our glasses to all that we find,
In horizons of stories, our hearts ever kind.
For in every twist, the laughter aligned,
In this world of wonder, we're wonderfully blind!

Lanterns Leading Through the Night

In the dark a lantern glows,
It flickers like a friendly nose.
I trip over roots and start to laugh,
My journey's a comedic photograph.

The shadows dance, they tease and play,
I wonder if they're lost today.
With giggles loud, I chase the breeze,
As if a clown slipped through the trees.

The moon's a joker, bright and round,
In its glow, my mishaps abound.
I wave goodbye to every fright,
And stroll along till morning light.

With every step, a riddle or two,
The night's a stage, and I'm the view.
A silly dance, a twirl, a spin,
Life is a jest, let the fun begin!

The Canvas on Which We Wander

A canvas spread, so vast and wide,
With splashes here, and colors tied.
I paint a sun with quite a grin,
And add in rain, to see where it's been.

With each bright stroke, a giggle's drawn,
I stumble over paint all gone.
My brush is wild, it jumps and skips,
An abstract trip with flailing hips.

Each corner's host to doodles bright,
Like stick figures on an awkward flight.
A wobbly road and shoes askew,
What fun we have in this colorful view!

As paint drips down, time warps and bends,
Around each twist, a laugh ascends.
The canvas laughs, it knows my aim,
With silly strokes, we share the fame!

Seeking Stars in Daylight

Under sun, we search for stars,
While busy dodging lunchroom sparrs.
We squint our eyes, we stretch our hands,
Trying to catch them in bandstands.

With a wink, one might appear,
A snack-sized star, a missed frontier.
We laugh aloud, the hunt's delight,
In broad daylight, they're out of sight!

Around the park, we dance and twirl,
With carts of dreams in every swirl.
Chasing light with ice cream cones,
Our giggles scattered like soft stones.

Fools we are, in sun's embrace,
Hunting stars in such a race.
But oh, the joy of this silly scheme,
The brightest stars live in our dream!

Unfolding the Map of Tomorrow

A map unfurls of crumpled dreams,
With spots that burst at the seams.
Here be hills, and there a lake,
I skip along for pure heart's sake.

The compass spins like a furry cat,
It points to places where I sat.
Each 'X' is marked with a birthday cake,
Wait, is that a mistake? Oh, for goodness' sake!

With every fold, a giggle's found,
Each twist of fate, a merry sound.
I'll laugh at paths I've yet to roam,
For in this map, I'll find my home!

Tomorrow's road will be a jest,
With silly signs that make me jest.
I'll dance my way through every quest,
And brush aside the unwanted stress!

Beneath the Surface of Tomorrow

In a world where socks often roam,
I search for purpose, far from home.
With cereal dreams, I make my stand,
Dancing with destiny's goofy hand.

Oh, the treasure maps of lost TV,
Suggesting paths where I might be.
A quest for meaning, or just a snack?
Who knows what's really on this track?

The clouds above giggle with glee,
As I chase my shadow and trip on a tree.
With spoons as swords, I take my flight,
Into a mystery, oh what a sight!

In the end, will I find the gold?
Or just a fridge with leftovers cold?
With laughter echoing, I will proceed,
For this odd journey is all I need.

The Map of Unwritten Stories

I found an old map, with Xs and dots,
It led to the kitchen and strange looking pots.
With spatulas wielded, I plotted my quest,
To uncover the secrets, oh what a jest!

The tales of the universe, I started to write,
In crayons and markers, a glorious sight.
The paper crumples, the ink surely fades,
But giggles sprinkle like confetti parades.

Magic exists in a dandelion's fluff,
As I chase after dreams, just never enough.
With a cap full of laughter and shoes full of fun,
I'll write my own stories, 'til the day is done.

Competitions with squirrels, I take on the day,
Who knew enlightenment was a game of play?
As I write my adventure in kitchen attire,
The map leads me back to my couch—what a fire!

Voices from the Unexplored

From the attic, strange whispers call me near,
Old toys with secrets, give a chuckle and cheer.
I grab my old blanket, my cape of great might,
To venture to lands only stars know at night.

The creatures I meet, oh what a delight,
With voices of giggles and snacks that feel right.
Together we plot to challenge the moon,
While debating if broccoli's a dish too immune.

The horizon beckons with laughter and fun,
Saying, "Join hands, oh why not, just run!"
As we leap through portals of giggly surprise,
I chase after dreams with wide-open eyes.

So, let's dance with shadows that slink and glide,
With socks on our hands, we'll take it in stride.
For though we may wander in search of the truth,
The silliness reigns, forever our youth.

Chasing Shadows of Meaning

With shadows like puppets, I set off to roam,
Through fields of confetti, my whimsical home.
Each step feels wobbly, my map is a plate,
Of pizza and laughter, I'd say it's first-rate.

Beneath the sun's smile, I skip and I sway,
While pondering secrets along the great way.
Each giggle a clue, each stumble a dance,
I dive into questions, all while in a trance.

With socks on my hands, I'm ready to go,
To chase the peculiar in the heart of the show.
What's the meaning, oh, I haven't a clue,
But I'll keep on searching, with ice cream too!

As evening draws near, shadows soften their play,
With pizza-stuffed stories, I'll call it a day.
For in the chase, joy is wrapped tight,
Unraveling laughter in the shimmering light.

Chasing the Unseen

I woke up late, forgot my shoe,
The map says 'go', but I haven't a clue.
With socks that mismatch, I step out the door,
Who knew the unknown would be such a chore?

A squirrel steals my sandwich, a bird sings a song,
I laugh with the neighbors, we all get along.
The street is a circus, with honks and a cheer,
The unseen is silly, yet I hold it near.

I dance with the breeze, strike a pose for the sun,
Tripped on my laces, this journey is fun.
With pockets of laughter, I'll gather the day,
Tomorrow I'll chase in a different way.

So here's to the chaos, the twists and the bends,
Who knew who could make such unruly friends?
We'll laugh at the madness, embrace all the flops,
Each step of the journey, until it all stops.

The Journey Beyond Self

They say find yourself, but where to begin?
I'm stuck in a tangle, my mind in a spin.
I trip on my thoughts, lose my way to the park,
Who knew self-discovery would leave such a mark?

With a paper map that's drawn in crayon,
I wander in circles, my logic all gone.
I bump into strangers, tell them my quest,
They laugh and they nod — I must be the best.

To search for oneself is a curious game,
I'm lost and I'm found, yet it's all the same.
I'll jump like a kangaroo, dance like a fool,
And figure it out — I've got my own rules.

The road is a riddle, with twists every turn,
I take notes in my head, but forget how to learn.
Yet laughter's my compass, my guide on this spree,
The unknown may frighten, but it's also quite free.

Collected Moments of Wonder

I stepped outside; the sky drew a grin,
With clouds shaped like puppies, an instant win!
I paused for a second, my coffee in hand,
What wonders await in this whimsical land?

An ant did a dance, a bird played a tune,
A pig in a tutu just flew by the moon.
I jotted it down, my notebook's afloat,
Collecting the moments like they were a boat.

Each smile that I meet feels like treasures in jars,
A wink from a stranger, a halt in the cars.
I capture the laughter, the quirks and the quirks,
In the gallery of life — how the magic works!

So here's to the wonders, both grand and the small,
The moments we gather are the best for us all.
I'll cherish these gems, each blink of delight,
In the zany parade of this silly old life.

Unraveled Threads of Destiny

They spun me a tale, with yarn of the best,
Of knots and of tangles, it put me to rest.
With threads that were frayed, I stitched up my fate,
What color will pop? Oh, just wait — it's too late!

I tied all my dreams to a kite on the hill,
Then tripped on my own feet and fell with a thrill.
The wind took a giggle, the kite soared away,
My plans are but whims — they're a game I can play.

The universe chuckles, it knows what I'll find,
With each twist and turn, I unstring my mind.
I dance with confusion, a waltz in the breeze,
These threads pull me closer, oh look, there's my cheese!

So raise up a toast to the knots yet to come,
For every lost dream brings new chances to hum.
In the whimsical journey of tangled delight,
I'll weave my own story, with laughter so bright.

Wandering Beyond the Horizon

I pack my bags with socks and snacks,
To find the joy in silly tracks,
A compass spins in dizzy glee,
As I chase the cat who runs from me.

Each step I take, a stumble near,
The world's a stage, I'm the engineer,
With maps that twist like licorice whips,
And all my dreams take funny trips.

I seek the treasure of lost old shoes,
In candy stores where I can't lose,
With giggles that echo, here and there,
I dance with clouds and flip my hair.

Beyond the hills, the laughter roams,
In every corner, joy finds homes,
As I skip and hop, oh, what a bliss,
Life's quirks unravel, all in a kiss.

Embracing the Unseen

I peek behind the curtains drawn,
Where dust bunnies have a cozy spawn,
With every laugh, a tickle grows,
In shadows where a funny bunny blows.

Invisible friends in hats so grand,
Crack jokes in ways I can't quite understand,
Each tickle fight is a bold embrace,
While I try to balance on my shoelace.

I hug the air, it's filled with cheer,
Pretending it whispers secrets near,
In life's unusual, quirky spree,
I find my joy in the mystery.

Under the stars, I spin around,
In a waltz with the unseen sound,
With giggles and whispers, the night does gleam,
In the wacky world where I can dream.

Destined for the Uncharted

With a silly map and a goofy grin,
I'm off to find where the fun begins,
Through caverns filled with candy dreams,
And fountain pools that burst with beams.

I trip on shoelaces tied too tight,
While chasing stars that dance at night,
In pickled ponds, where frogs teach me,
To bounce around, wild and free.

Through jungle paths of giggles and sighs,
I stumble over my own two thighs,
With each misstep, new joys appear,
As I embrace the whims of cheer.

The world unfolds as I try to glide,
In a comical twist, I take it in stride,
Each corner turned, a fortune found,
In uncharted laughs, I'm forever bound.

Navigating the Veil of Dreams

In dreams, I sail on ships of cheese,
With ice cream waves and laughing breeze,
Mice, they pilot while I dance,
On shiny clouds, I take my chance.

Through fields of jellybeans I roam,
With each sweet step, I feel at home,
I ride on unicorns, silly and bright,
In the starry carnival of the night.

I catch the moon in a zingy jar,
As wishes bloom like a sweet bazaar,
With every giggle, the stars align,
On this wacky path, I sip my wine.

In chatter with shadows, I find delight,
As dreams unfold into playful flight,
While navigating this comical stream,
I float through life, caught in a dream.

The Canvas of Hidden Dreams

With paintbrush in hand, I start to play,
The colors of hope spill bright every day.
Sometimes I just mix a little too much,
End up with a shade that can barely be touched.

I dance on the canvas, who knows what I'll find,
A unicorn here, oh look, a kangaroo blind!
Each stroke a wild tale from dreams tucked away,
Perhaps I should stick to my day job, they say.

A tap on the shoulder, a laugh from behind,
It's my inner child, seeking peace of mind.
Together we giggle, we plot and we scheme,
Transforming our chaos into a wild dream.

So paint me a picture, oh wonderful fate,
Where ducks hold the keys to the secrets of great.
In this vibrant world, forever I'll roam,
Creating my future, I'm always at home.

The Echoing Silence of Purpose

In the quiet of night, when thoughts start to squawk,
With echoes of 'Why?' that just love to mock.
I search for the meaning, it's quite the wild chase,
Only to find it's just my cat's funny face.

Whispers of wisdom float through the air,
Yet often they vanish without a care.
The universe giggles, it's all in good fun,
As I play hide and seek with the ultimate pun.

A map made of riddles, a puzzle unspooled,
The answers are there, just look, you old fool!
With each twist and turn, my laughter will rise,
For the quest is a joy, and a clever disguise.

So dance through the echoes, don't take it too hard,
The silence is loud, but the journey's a bard.
With each whispered question, a chuckle evolves,
In the maze of this life, we're the curious solves.

Everflowing Springs of Potential

Imagine a spring that bubbles with cheer,
Potential so rich, it tickles your ear.
I dive in headfirst, with a splash and a grin,
Only to find that I forgot how to swim.

In the rippling waters, reflections collide,
Like two clowns in a car taking joyrides wide.
What's brewing beneath? A soup of success?
Or just a few fish and a whole lot of mess?

A dip in my dreams, oh the wild things I'll see,
With mermaids that sing, come join in with me!
They strut and they shimmy, quite the vibrant crew,
While I try to remember what day it is too.

So splash in your spring, let your worries all flow,
Embrace the absurd, let your true colors show.
With fountains of laughter that never run dry,
It's the journey that matters, not the by and by.

Labyrinths of the Soul

In the maze of my mind, where the hallways twist,
I stumble and dance, can't resist this absurd list.
With signs pointing nowhere, it's quite a delight,
I lose track of hours, but hey, what's the fright?

There's a sock here, a donut—what have we found?
Perhaps the exit is where silliness abounds.
I giggle and wiggle, lose myself in the fray,
Every turn leads to laughter, come what may.

The walls whisper jokes, they crack up a storm,
As I frolic through corners, I quest to transform.
With each silly step, my spirit takes flight,
In this labyrinth wonder, I'm dancing all night.

So follow the giggles, let whimsy prevail,
In the twists and the turns, we shall not derail.
For in every small detour, joy takes its toll,
Embrace the confusion, our labyrinth's whole.

www.ingramcontent.com/pod-product-compliance
Lightning Source LLC
Chambersburg PA
CBHW071815160426
43209CB00003B/99